curiou$about

PANDAS

BY AMY S. HANSEN

AMICUS • AMICUS INK

What are you

CHAPTER TWO

2

Panda Behavior
PAGE
10

CHAPTER ONE

1

Life as a Panda
PAGE
4

curious about?

CHAPTER THREE

3

Panda Families
PAGE
16

Curious About is published
by Amicus and Amicus Ink
P.O. Box 227
Mankato, MN 56002
www.amicuspublishing.us

Copyright © 2023 Amicus.
International copyright reserved in all countries.
No part of this book may be reproduced in any
form without written permission from the publisher.

Designer: Aubrey Harper
Photo researcher: Bridget Prehn
Editor: Alissa Thielges
Series designer: Kathleen Petelinsek

Library of Congress Cataloging-in-Publication Data
Names: Hansen, Amy, author. Title: Curious about pandas
/ Amy S. Hansen Description: Mankato, MN : Amicus,
[2023] | Series: Curious about wild animals | Includes
bibliographical references and index. | Audience:
Ages 6–9 | Audience: Grades 2–3 Identifiers: LCCN
2019056834 (print) | LCCN 2019056835 (ebook)
| ISBN 9781645491354 (library binding) | ISBN
9781681527024 (paperback) | ISBN 9781645491774
(pdf) Subjects: LCSH: Pandas—Juvenile literature. | Giant
panda—Juvenile literature. Classification: LCC QL737.
C27 H3918 2023 (print) | LCC QL737.C27 (ebook) |
DDC 599.789—dc23 LC record available at
https://lccn.loc.gov/2019056834
LC ebook record available at
https://lccn.loc.gov/2019056835

Photos © iStock/BirdImages cover, 1; Alamy/Hung
Chung Chih 2 (left), 7; Shutterstock/clkraus 2 (right),
10–11; Alamy/Steve Bloom Images 3, 18; Shutterstock/i
viewfinder 5 (top photo); Wikimedia/USDA 5 (fish);
iStock/ruiruito 5 (bug); iStock/Antonel 5 (bamboo);
PublicDomainPictures.net/Petr Kratochvil 5 (apple);
Shutterstock/Tsekhmister 5 (mouse); FreeVectorMaps.
com 6; Alamy/Arco Images/GmbH 8–9; Shutterstock/
Hung Chung Chih 13; Alamy/ Philippe Lejeanvre 14–15;
Alamy/National Geographic Image Collection 16;
Alamy/Nature Picture Library 17; Alamy/Steve Bloom
Images 19; Pexels/Flickr 20; iStock/GlobalP 21 (panda);
Shutterstock/Anan Kaewkhammul 21 (Asian black);
Shutterstock/Svetlana Foote 21 (American black); Shutter-
stock/Daria Rybakova 21 (brown); Shutterstock/Sergey
Uryadnikov 21 (polar); Flat Icon/Flat Iron/Freepik 22 and
23 (paw icon); iStock/lumpynoodles
22 and 23 (bear icon)

Bear Sizes 21
Stay Curious! Learn More . . .22
Glossary 24
Index 24

What do pandas eat?

Pandas are picky eaters. They eat **bamboo** and more bamboo. They can eat 40 pounds (18 kg) of bamboo a day. That's a lot of bamboo! As bears, they can also eat insects and small animals. But they much prefer bamboo. It is easier to find and tastes better.

Pandas eat the leaves, shoots, and roots of bamboo.

1% — 99%

PANDA DIET

Pandas eat 99% bamboo and 1% fruit, bugs, fish, and mice.

Where do wild pandas live?

Giant pandas live in the mountains of China. They live in forests and make dens in tree stumps. Bamboo is everywhere. There are only about 1,900 giant pandas in the wild. They used to live in more areas. But humans destroyed their **habitat**. Most of it is now farmland. Panda forests are now protected.

DID YOU KNOW?
Pandas can live 20 years in the wild.

■ Past Panda Range
■ Current Panda Range

Pandas
are great
climbers.

The color pattern of panda fur is unique.

Why are pandas black and white?

We don't know. One guess is safety. The black fur lets them hide in the shadows. The white fur blends in with snow. Another guess is community. Pandas need to know other pandas. They look for black and white markings.

CHAPTER TWO

PANDA BEHAVIOR

What do pandas like to do?

Pandas sleep two to four hours at a time, then go back to eating.

Most of the time, pandas eat and sleep. Pandas eat 12 or more hours a day. Unlike other bears, they do not **hibernate**. They are built for cold weather. Their fur is thick. It keeps them warm. Pandas love the snow.

Do pandas play?

Yes! Panda cubs love to play. They run and climb. Adults are more serious. But that changes when it snows. Then both adults and cubs play. Pandas roll around in the snow and slide down hills.

Panda cubs tumble
and play together.

Do pandas talk to each other?

Yes. Adult pandas chirp, honk, and bark. They also "talk" through scent. Pandas can smell really well. Female pandas smell different than males. When it is time to **mate**, males sniff out the females.

Two panda cubs talk and play in a tree.

Do pandas live together?

Bamboo forests can easily hide pandas.

No. Adult pandas like to live alone. Each one has a 2-mile (3.2-km) piece of the forest. It is their **territory**. Pandas mark the land with their scent. This warns other pandas to stay away.

This panda pees on a tree
to mark it with its scent.

What are panda cubs like?

A panda has one or two cubs at a time.

Cubs are born very small. They are about as long as a pencil. But they grow quickly. Cubs are fluffy and curious. They love to roll around and climb things. They wrestle with mom and learn to pick bamboo. After about 2 years, a cub leaves its mother. It finds its own territory.

Three-month old panda

Are there other kinds of pandas?

Red pandas also eat bamboo.

Yes. There are small red pandas. They live in China, too. Giant pandas were named after them. People thought the two **species** looked alike. But they aren't related. Giant pandas are bears. Red pandas are cousins of raccoons.

GIANT PANDA

200 POUNDS (91 KG)

ASIAN
BLACK BEAR

300 POUNDS (136 KG)

AMERICAN
BLACK BEAR

400 POUNDS (181 KG)

BROWN BEAR

700 POUNDS (318 KG)

POLAR BEAR

1,000 POUNDS (454 KG)

BEAR SIZES

ASK MORE QUESTIONS

How many pandas live in zoos?

Are wild panda populations getting bigger?

Try a BIG QUESTION:
How do pandas help other animals and plants in their habitat?

SEARCH FOR ANSWERS

Search the library catalog or the Internet.
A librarian, teacher, or parent can help you.

Using Keywords
Find the looking glass.

Keywords are the most important words in your question.

?

If you want to know about:

- pandas living in zoos, type: PANDAS IN ZOOS

- if panda populations are rising, type: WILD PANDA POPULATION

FIND GOOD SOURCES

Here are some good, safe sources you can use in your research.

Your librarian can help you find more.

Books

All About Asian Giant Pandas by Carol Kline, 2019.

Pandas by Julie Murray, 2020.

Internet Sites

Nat Geo Kids | 10 Facts about Pandas!

www.natgeokids.com/za/discover/animals/general-animals/ten-panda-facts

National Geographic is a respected news organization. It reports on nature and animals.

San Diego Zoo Kids | Giant Panda
https://sdzwildlifeexplorers.org/animals/giant-panda

The San Diego Zoo is a respected U.S. zoo. It funds research to help save animals.

Every effort has been made to ensure that these websites are appropriate for children. However, because of the nature of the Internet, it is impossible to guarantee that these sites will remain active indefinitely or that their contents will not be altered.

SHARE AND TAKE ACTION

Visit bears at a zoo.
Read about their size, habitat, and diet. How are they different from pandas?

Virtually adopt a panda through a wildlife organization.
Your money may protect pandas' habitat.

Watch a webcam that shows pandas living in a zoo.
How do they act? Compare with what you have read.

GLOSSARY

bamboo A type of grass with woody stems.

habitat The natural environment where an animal lives.

hibernate When an animal goes into a deep sleep to survive the winter because there is a lack of food.

mate When a male and female come together to make a baby.

species A group of living things with similar features that are grouped under a common name, such as bears.

territory The area an animal considers to be his or her home.

INDEX

bears 4, 11, 20, 21
colors 9
communication 15, 16
cubs 12, 19
food 4, 5, 6
fur 9, 11
habitat 6
life span 6
mating 15
playing 12, 19
populations 6
red pandas 20
scent marking 16
size 19, 21
sleep 11
territories 16, 19

About the Author

Amy S. Hansen lives with her husband, two sons and a dog in Maryland. She has also lived in Wisconsin, Ohio and Michigan. One of her favorite parts of her job is doing research and finding out fun facts. Those facts made these books very fun to write.